Kiri
in the Classroom

Jamie McPartland

illustrations by Aleksandra Fabia

Copyright © Jamie McPartland 2021
Aleph Editing and Montessori Learners
www.alephediting.com

All rights reserved. No part of this book may be reproduced, stored in a retrieval system, or transmitted in any form or by any means, electronic, mechanical, photocopying, recording, or otherwise, without the prior written permission of the author, except as provided by U.S.A. copyright law.

The Library of Congress has catalogued this hardcover edition as follows:
McPartland, Jamie, author
Kiri in the Classroom / by Jamie McPartland; illustrated by Aleksandra Fabia. — 1st ed.
p.   cm.
Summary: 4-year-old Kiri spends her first day at a Montessori school, welcomed by a friendly guide and classmates.

ISBN 978-0-578-93329-0

This morning is Kiri's first morning at school. Although she is a tiny bit nervous, she's also very excited, and feeling very ready.

When she walks through the front door of her school, a woman with a friendly face calls out Kiri's name. "Hello Kiri, you're in the Owl class, with me!"

The woman holds out her hand for Kiri to shake. "Do you remember me, Kiri? I'm Autumn, your guide."
"Yes," Kiri says, even though she doesn't remember Autumn very well from when she visited the school.
"Our classroom is just this way." Autumn's eyes have a warm twinkle in them, which reminds Kiri of her papa.

Kiri follows Autumn into her classroom.
"I'll be right back," Autumn says. "There are other children for me to welcome. There are many older kids here who would be happy to help you as you settle in."

Just inside the classroom door there is a long row of cubbies where kids are hanging up their jackets and backpacks, and taking off their outdoor shoes. One older boy is wearing a rainbow shirt—Kiri loves it!

"How do I know which cubby is mine?" Kiri asks the boy with the rainbow shirt.
"It will have your name on it," says the boy with a smile.

Kiri doesn't know how to read but she knows her name starts with a letter shaped like K—kih. But she sees two cubbies with the letter K. Which one is mine? she wonders.

The boy with the rainbow shirt says, "Do you need help?" and he reads the names that start with the letter K—kih—to her.
"Kobe," he reads, "and Kiri."
"Kiri! That's me!" Kiri says.

The boy smiles at her. "Your backpack goes on this hook...and your shoes go down here."

Kiri puts her things exactly where they go and slips on her brand new indoor shoes, which have stars and the moon on them.

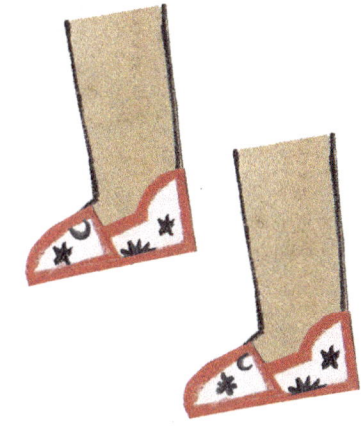

In the classroom, there are colorful flags hanging along the shelves, and bouquets of fresh flowers. There are pots with small plants in them on the windowsills and a glass bowl with a fish in it. On the shelves, there are all kinds of beautiful and interesting projects in baskets: puzzles and games, drawing and painting supplies, brightly painted blocks and beads. Kiri wants to pick up all of them!

The older kids are busy moving around the room and they all seem to know what to do. Kiri has no idea what she should be doing.

But then Autumn's voice calls out, "Good morning everyone. We're going to start the day by gathering together. Everyone come and join me on the oval rug!"

Kiri goes along with the other kids to the rug and they all sit together in a giant oval. Kiri looks at all of the kids' faces. There are a lot of older kids but also a few her own age. One kid is wearing a necklace with banana-colored beads. Another kid has all of her fingers linked together on her lap like shoelaces.

"Now it's time for roll call," says Autumn. "We will roll the ball, and when it comes to you, you say your name so everyone can hear it."

First the ball rolls to a boy wearing socks that don't match. "Malik," he says. Everybody begins to sing:

*Hello, Malik, Hello, Malik
How are you? How are you?
We're so glad to have you,
We're so glad to have you.
Here at school, here at school.

* Sung to the melody of "Frere Jacques."

Then Malik rolls the ball to a girl who is picking her nose. "Juniper," she says. Everybody, including Kiri, sings the song with Juniper's name. She rolls the ball straight to Kiri. "Kiri," she says but not very loudly.

Everyone sings:

Hello, Kiri, Hello, Kiri
How are you? How are you?
We're so glad to have you,
We're so glad to have you.
Here at school, here at school

Then Kiri rolls the ball to the boy across from her— the boy with the rainbow shirt. His name is Leo.

After a story and a song on the rug, the kids get up one at a time and spread out around the room to do different types of projects. Autumn asks Kiri, "Would you like to come with me and see an activity I think you might like?"

Kiri follows Autumn to one of the shelves. On the shelf, Autumn shows Kiri a tray with a towel, a sponge, and several small bird sculptures on it.

"Can I show you this washing activity?" Autumn asks Kiri. Kiri nods her head yes.

Miss Autumn carries the tray to a small table by the windows. "I'm putting the tray down here for you," Autumn tells Kiri. "Everything you need to wash these birds is right here on the tray. We'll just need to fill this bowl with soap and water for you."

Kiri looks at everything on the tray, especially the bird sculptures, which are a little dirty. One bird is blue, one is pink, and one is orange. Kiri picks one of the birds up. It's the perfect size for her hand!

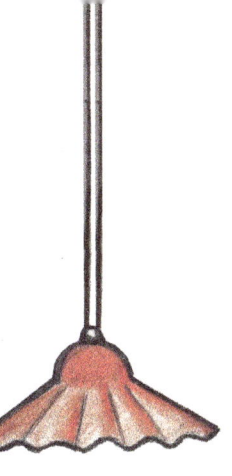

"Does this look like something you want to try?" Autumn asks Kiri. Kiri smiles. "Yes! I love animals, especially birds and cats," Kiri says. Autumn smiles back and tells Kiri, "Why don't I show you how we do this kind of work then."

First, Autumn shows Kiri where her apron is so Kiri's clothes won't get wet.

"Once the birds are completely clean, here is a towel to dry them. If you need anything, one of the older children can help you, and I'll be just over there," Autumn says.

Kiri feels happy washing the birds by the window. When she looks out the window onto the school garden, she sees the plants swaying gently in a breeze. The classroom, Kiri thinks, feels like a cozy nest full of fun work to do, safe and warm.

When Kiri is done washing the birds, and drying them with the towel, Autumn comes and shows Kiri how to dump out the dirty water, put the towel in the laundry bin, and then put the tray back on the shelf. Kiri puts her apron away all by herself.

"Did you know that we have real living creatures that we take care of here at school?" Autumn asks Kiri.

"What kind?" Kiri asks.

"Well we have the fish of course, but the creatures I'm talking about live in the garden. They're worms!"

"Wow!" Kiri says. "What do worms eat?"

"They eat scraps of food from our kitchen, like apple cores and eggshells. Would you like to feed them?"

"Yes!" says Kiri.

Autumn asks Leo, the boy in the rainbow shirt, to show Kiri how to grind up eggshells for the worms to eat. Leo seems excited to show Kiri.

"This is one of my favorite things to do," Leo tells Kiri. He suggests doing this work cross-legged on a work mat on the floor. Together they roll out a work mat, then Leo shows Kiri which shelf the mortar and pestle are on. Kiri carries the mortar and the pestle to her work mat, then they go together to the kitchen and collect broken eggshells from a basket.

"This stone you hold is the pestle. You put the eggshells in the stone bowl and use the pestle to break the eggshells into tiny pieces. Worms are small and this way the eggshells will be just the size of their tiny mouths."

Soon Kiri herself is crushing eggshells with the mortar and pestle. It's very satisfying. Crunch-crunch-clurk-crunch goes the pestle.

When Kiri is done, Leo goes with her to the cubbies so they can put on their outdoor shoes and go to the garden. Kiri looks at the names above the cubbies and sees the letter K—kih. This time, she knows which cubby is hers because she sees her coat and her backpack there.

"Ready?" Leo asks with a big smile.
"Ready!" says Kiri.

A few kids are already out in the garden working. The garden smells lovely, like sweet katsura leaves.

"Where are the worms?" asks Kiri.
"They're here, in this box," says Leo and he lifts the lid of a wooden box.

Inside, there is dirt, bits of paper, and fruit and vegetable peels. Kiri and Leo put their hands into the box to move the compost around. Now Kiri can see them: small, wiggling pink worms.

"Some people think worms are gross," Leo says to Kiri. "But I think they're adorable."
"I like 'em too," Kiri says. "They have a really big family."
Leo laughs. "Yeah, there are a hundred brothers and sisters! And a mom and dad in there somewhere, of course."

Suddenly Kiri realizes she misses her mama and papa. She's having fun at school, but she also wonders when she'll see them again.

"Do you ever miss your parents when you're at school?" Kiri asks Leo.

"Oh yeah, I miss them sometimes, but I know I'll see them soon and I like being with all of the kids in our class. They're kind of like my family too."

Kiri likes Leo's answer. Maybe the kids in her class and their guide Autumn are sort of like a school family.

"You can miss people you love and also have fun at the same time," Leo says.

Kiri sprinkles the crushed eggshells she's prepared throughout the box with her fingers.

"When will the worms eat them?" Kiri asks since the worms don't seem to be that excited about the eggshells.
"I don't know," Leo says, "maybe after we put the lid back on the box."

Once they close the worm box, Kiri looks around at the garden. There are grapevines and flowers, and pumpkins growing under big shady leaves.

"Wanna try a cherry tomato?" one of the kids asks her. Kiri does. It's juicy and sweet.

Then she and Leo pluck grapes off the grapevines.
"Wow!" Kiri says, "It tastes just like a mouthful of juice!"

Soon it will be lunchtime, and then naptime. Soon Kiri's papa will arrive with the bicycle to pick Kiri up and she will tell him all about her day. For now, Kiri is happy to be in the sweet-smelling garden with her new friends and the big family of worms munching away in their worm box. On this, her first morning at school, Kiri feels there is an important spot for her in her new school family.

Jamie McPartland is a writer and editor living in Portland, Oregon. With an MFA in Creative Writing from The New School and a background in education, she directs her literary passion into producing beautiful collaborative book projects. The text for the Kiri book series is inspired by life with her daughter, Oksana.

Aleksandra Fabia is a visual artist and illustrator based in Krakow, Poland. She is Founder of a non-profit for the promotion of children's literature, and was a finalist in the Illustrators Exhibition of the 2021 Bologna Children's Book Fair.

The support and spirit of the following people lifted this book off the ground: Brian and Joyce McPartland, Peter Oviatt, and the Portland, Oregon Montessori community.

CPSIA information can be obtained
at www.ICGtesting.com
Printed in the USA
BVHW021052130922
646892BV00007B/479